The Artisans

OBJECTS TALK BACK

About This Book Series

In collaboration with the Ethnologisches Museum and the Museum für Asiatische Kunst of the Staatliche Museen zu Berlin, the Stiftung Humboldt Forum im Berliner Schloss invited the writer Priya Basil to curate a series of events and books: *Objects Talk Back*.

Every year, Priya Basil asks two writers to engage with an object of their choice—either from the exhibited collection or from the museums' storage depots.

The project represents a new curatorial practice (complementing ongoing provenance research) characterized by transparency and dialogue regarding the collections in the Humboldt Forum, the complex history of its location and entanglements with contemporary global issues. The aim is to investigate the provenance history of the objects while simultaneously engaging in a direct dialogue with people biographically connected to the countries of origin, thereby fostering international multivocality and transforming museum practices.

Madeleine Thien

The Artisans

HUMBOLDT FORUM

DIAPHANES

Three Uyghur Princes, III 6876 a
Mural painting, pigments on mud plaster
Cave 20 (Grünwedel's numbering 9), Bezeklik, Xinjiang, China
10th/11th century
59.5 × 62.4 cm
Museum für Asiatische Kunst – Staatliche Museen zu Berlin

This particularly well-preserved and thus most renowned donor portrait of Uyghur-Buddhist art was brought to Berlin with the collection of the second Turfan expedition (October 1904 – December 1905). German explorers and archaeologists had traveled to Xinjiang, where they collected Buddhist artworks and manuscripts and took them to Germany. The finds provided significant insights into the cultural history of the region, but today they are critically reassessed within the debate on colonial appropriation.

The painting depicts three men wearing Uyghur hats and with carefully plaited, long black hair. Their side-slit robes reveal black riding boots. This type of clothing indicates that nomadic traditions continued despite a sedentary lifestyle.

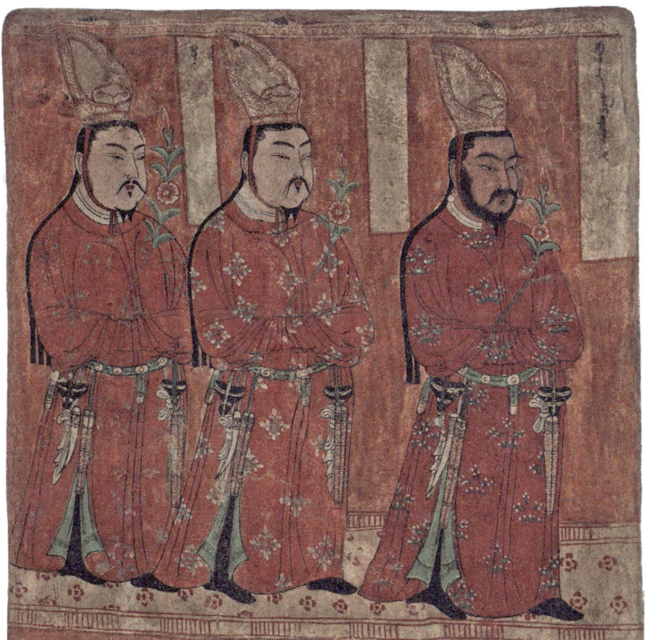

OBJECTS TALK BACK

Objects have voices, which we may not hear. Literature helps us to listen.

Objects Talk Back is a project that asks: what are the possibilities of literature to open up new stories, questions and relations when writers engage with museum archives?

While there are promising currents of change, ethnological museum collections remain tied to violent colonial histories and ongoing practices of domination. Information for most objects is still limited to date of creation or acquisition, place of origin, type of material, collector or donator. Even these details are not always accurate.

The archaeologist Dan Hicks proposes "necrography," a practice of digging into the past to trace the colonial story behind an object.[1] Such an approach may reveal much of value, but also leave one "straining against the limits of the archive," as literary scholar Saidiya Hartman writes.[2]

Colonial archives contain their own prejudices and distortions. Hartman suggests "critical fabulation"—melding history, theory and fiction—"to displace the received or authorized account." Inspired by these ideas, I coined the term "fabulography" for *Objects Talk Back*. In a piece for *British Art Studies*, I describe fabulography as an invitation to work creatively with-from-through gaps, facts and imagination to expand the narrative space around an object.[3] Fabulography involves digging deep, uncovering painful details, but also rising up, celebrating, honoring, reconnecting.

Since 2021, two writers are invited each year to explore collections of the Ethnologisches Museum and the Museum für Asiatische Kunst, both part of the Staatliche Museen zu Berlin. The writers encounter objects displayed in the Humboldt Forum, Berlin, and also those stored in the museums' depots. They select an object, and respond however they wish—through fiction, poetry, narrative nonfiction, multimedia texts. Later, they present the finished work at a live event in the Humboldt

Forum. Now, objects talk back in a book series as well, affirming Hartman's appeal "to consider stories as a form of compensation, perhaps the only kind we will ever receive."[4]

Priya Basil

1 Dan Hicks, "Necrography: Death-Writing in the Colonial Museum," *British Art Studies*, Issue 19, 2021: https://doi.org/10.17658/issn.2058-5462/issue-19/conversation. | **2** Saidiya Hartman, "Venus in Two Acts," *Small Axe* (Indiana University) 12, no. 2 (2008): https://muse.jhu.edu/search?action=browse&limit=publisher_id:3 (accessed March 9, 2024). | **3** Priya Basil, "Writing to Life," *British Art Studies*, Issue 19, 2021: https://www.britishartstudies.ac.uk/issues/issue-index/issue-19/death-writing-in-the-colonial-museums (accessed March 9, 2024). | **4** Hartman, "Venus in Two Acts."

Priya Basil

Introduction

"It is one thing to suffer, another to be forgotten ... we will not be abandoned by history,"[1] writes Madeleine Thien in her novel *Do Not Say We Have Nothing*. Her entire oeuvre might be summarized with those lines. Through novels, short stories, essays and plays, she has examined the darkest reaches of authoritarianism, what it destroys and what survives its merciless machinations. Thien grapples with some of the hardest and most haunting questions: What can be redeemed when all seems lost? Who are we—who can we become—with-without-for each other? How can more promising worlds be shaped from painful knowledge?

Thien's writing affirms the enduring intimacy of history: "The things you experience are written on your cells as memories and patterns, which are reprinted again on the next generation."[2] *Do Not Say We Have Nothing* unfolds in present-day Vancouver and in twentieth-century China, from the time of the Cultural Revolution to the events in Tiananmen Square. The historical characters seek to preserve a book of records that holds the most personal tales of that tumultuous time, which the state sought to dominate with a single narrative. To keep alive a polyphony of voices, a multiplicity of stories becomes a profound form of resistance. "All we have on this earth, all we are, is a record."[3] Each record is unique, cherished, worthy of care. This is what Thien seeks to honor through beautiful language, expansive imagination and love. In her work, every sentence becomes an act of remembrance, every individual story a memorial.

In *Dogs at the Perimeter*, her novel set partly in Cambodia during the regime of the Khmer Rouge, Thien writes: "Belongings were slid away, then family, then loved ones, and then finally our loyalties and ourselves. Worthless or precious, indifferent or loved, all of our treasures had been treated the same."[4] The task of literature is the exact opposite—to treat each and every one as if they may restore the whole.

Immersive research in the places she writes of, as well as in libraries and archives, has always been central to Thien's writing practice. She has traveled extensively in

China, Cambodia and other parts of South East and Central Asia. Her deep knowledge of these regions was the foundation from which she approached *Objects Talk Back*. While touring the Humboldt Forum with her partner, the writer Rawi Hage, and curator Lilla Russell-Smith, she became intrigued by objects that came to Berlin via collections from the Turfan expeditions (1902–1914), from the region of the Northern Silk Road (present-day Xinjiang Uyghur Autonomous Region). Thien was especially drawn to paintings connected with a Buddhist cave temple in Bezeklik, the exquisite contents of which, as Thien describes in the afterword to her story, are forever lost; today, we only know them through sketches, photographs and a few small fragments. The wall painting which so moved her, and which inspired *The Artisans*, is an image of three Uyghur princes, donors who contributed to the construction of a grotto in the Bezeklik Thousand Buddha Caves. The painting would have hung on one side of the entrance into the cave's inner chamber.

Madeleine Thien was born in Vancouver, Canada, to a Malaysian Chinese father and a Hong Kong Chinese mother. She is the author of five books of fiction, most recently *The Book of Records* (2025), a novel that carries the same name as the fictional tome in *Do Not Say We Have Nothing*. An opera, *Chinatown*, created by Thien with composer Alice Ping Yee Ho and writer Paul Yee, is in development. She has received Canada's highest literary honors, including the Governor General's Literary Award for Fiction. Her work has been internationally celebrated, shortlisted for awards including the Booker Prize and the Women's Prize for Fiction, and her books have been translated into more than twenty-five languages. She has been awarded numerous stipends and fellowships, including from the Cullman Center for Scholars and Writers in New York and the Borchard Foundation. She has taught literature and fiction in Canada, Hong Kong, Germany, Nigeria, the United States, Zimbabwe and Singapore.

The Artisans is at once a story of impermanence and continuity, embodying the Buddhist world it depicts. Loss permeates the narrative, quietly yet inescapably haunting its edges through the absence of loved ones whose disappearance is evoked but never explained: "he used to have a daughter and three sons, and all of them were taken away."[5] Different characters, similar stories: "my sister and mother died three years ago." Old and young are equally afflicted: "He had no one to say goodbye to, no parents, no brothers or sisters, not even a stray cat." Personal calamities echo wider cataclysms yet to come, or perhaps the fact that all tragedies are happening or have already happened, somewhere. Time always circles in Thien's writing. And however dark the passages, there is also wonder, delight, joy. So we climb up and down the mountain with two young boys, Khirs and Nestis, sent by the master painter on an impossible mission to find the most elusive colors and the most unusual faces. Excited, energetic, they find these and more, pulling us most surprisingly into the world of the three donors.

"A story is a shifting creature, an eternal mirror that catches our lives at unexpected angles."[6] Like the artisans she depicts, Thien "lights the underlying layers with a memory world."[7] Thus, she takes us into the dreams of the boys, then deep into the cave before its destruction, to an "inner room [which] holds, beneath a dome, a sculpture and an image of the Avalokiteshvara Buddha. Bey Sahi asks me who I think Avalokiteshvara is. Of course, being my father's son, this is an easy question. 'Avalokiteshvara is the emanation of compassion in this world.'"

After reading Thien's story, Lilla Russell-Smith, Curator of Central Asian Art at the Museum für Asiatische Kunst, responded by email: "you have soaked up so much information in such a short time, and put it through the prism of your amazing imagination, that something very remarkable and new has been created, I am very moved, and would like to thank you for this from my heart. Every time I read your short story I discover something new." In an afterword to *The Artisans*, Thien acknowledges her debt to Russell-Smith's research, in particular her book *Uygur Patronage in Dunhuang.* Such mutual inspiration, such reciprocity between a writer and curator is rare and special. Lilla Russell-Smith offered to host the event with Thien and Hage within the exhibition space and to change one display in honor of Thien's text. Both of these gestures are a first for the *Objects Talk Back* project.

Russell-Smith wrote to Thien:

"I spoke to the chief conservator Toralf Gabsch and the designer Britta Paulich, and despite their enormous workload ... they have kindly agreed to make my dream

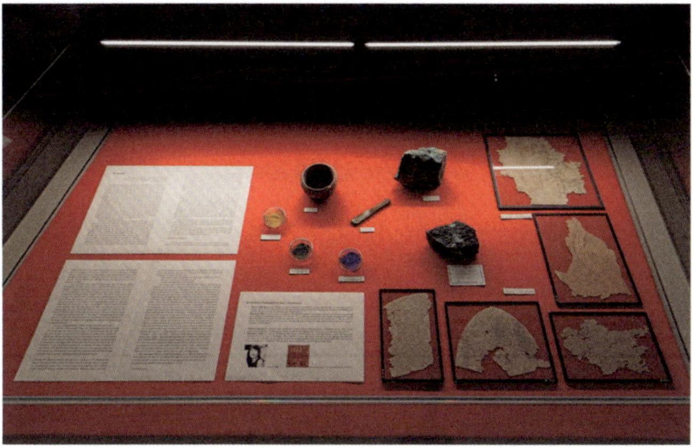

The display case was changed in honor of Madeleine Thien's text.
Museum für Asiatische Kunst – Staatliche Museen zu Berlin, 2023

possible in this super short time. We are going to take out the manuscripts in the display case under the projection (these are due to be changed in any case) and will replace them with:

1. on one side a part of your text printed (with labels explaining why this is exhibited)

2. on the other side three stencils—one came to my mind straight away reading your text—with the slender hands and face of *Avalokiteshvara with a Thousand Hands and Thousand Eyes* and with a bowl made of wood—with remains of green color on it, and possibly also colors or

minerals like malachite—I am going to see what Toralf Gabsch has in his workshop on Wednesday.

I hope you like this idea."

Thien replied: "I love these ideas for *The Artisans*—it's incredible that the story fragments can be placed in the display case. I love the objects you have chosen, the stencils, the wooden bowl, and the pigments. I cannot wait to see them."[8]

"Fragments" became the title Hage and Thien selected for their joint event, where Hage would read an essay responding to his chosen object—the "fragmented leaves" of a Manichaean manuscript from the same region as the painting behind Thien's story. "The experience of encounter always remakes us," both authors reflected after their work for *Objects Talk Back*. In the most profound encounters, the sense of transformation is mutual. "I have also been changed in the process," Russell-Smith said. "Somehow meeting you both and reading *Do Not Say We Have Nothing* sharpened my own focus, and has helped me to plan my work for the next years." She intends to center her future work around fragments.

"Today, most Uyghurs are Muslims. For centuries, however, Uyghurs were Buddhists," according to the scholar Johan Elverskog. His book *A History of Uyghur Buddhism* shows how Uyghurs "stood at the center of Buddhist Eurasia, linking far-flung regions and traditions."[9] Thien's story recreates that era and anticipates its end. Elverskog's book indicates that, "as Muslim power grew, Uyghur Buddhists converted to Islam, rewriting their past and erasing their Buddhist history." Some erasures happen organically, some violently. Thien's work is dedicated to distinguishing between such currents, between what is chosen, what is imposed and the delicate space between. The fate of the Uyghur people includes all kinds of erasures. In her afterword, Thien recognizes this and points the reader to sources documenting ongoing human rights violations against Uyghurs in the Xinjiang Autonomous Region.

In *The Artisans*, as in all Thien's writing, we find the most intimate human wish, the deepest promise of literature: "have faith that, one day, someone else will keep the record."[10]

1 Madeleine Thien, *Do Not Say We Have Nothing* (London: Granta Publications, 2016), pp. 178–79. | **2** Ibid., p. 235. | **3** Ibid. | **4** Madeleine Thien, *Dogs at the Perimeter* (Toronto: McClelland & Stewart, 2011), p. 39. | **5** All quotes in this paragraph from Thien, *The Artisans*. | **6** Thien, *Do Not Say We Have Nothing*, p. 415. | **7** Thien, *The Artisans* (this and the following quote). | **8** Email exchange between Lilla Russell-Smith and Madeleine Thien, October 2, 2023. | **9** Johan Elverskog, *A History of Uyghur Buddhism* (New York: Columbia University Press, 2024), https://cup.columbia.edu/book/a-history-of-uyghur-buddhism/9780231215251/. **10** Thien, *Do Not Say We Have Nothing*, p. 418.

Madeleine Thien

The Artisans

Two boys play in the high river valley of the Bezeklik, the place of paintings, outside the Uyghur imperial city of Kocho. There's the river, and beyond the river, the mountains. The sky is a deep azure.

On the morning that the princes of the Sahi family are expected to visit the site, Father sends Nestis and me out for materials. The workshop wants us gone. Uncle Rangkar says we are loose talkers. Cousin Ping says our horsing around scares the monks. "I think the problem," my father explains, "is that you forget this sanctuary is their home, not yours." "You're servants, in other words," says Tejin. "Shut it," says Uncle Rangkar, "or we'll kick you out, too." Tejin smirks and keeps painting. He has his shirt off and is working on the necklace of a prince who kneels to offer up a tray of big fat grapes. Nestis and I don't waste time arguing. We're twelve years old, swift as

Ferghana horses, and we feel on top of the world as we hurtle downhill to the painters' village. We're out of breath when we get there, mostly from shouting the whole way. We're also sweating buckets. My father is clever: Nestis and I study the packets of clay, pigment and paper he wants us to match, and are impressed by his sneakiness. He's set us an obstacle course: tracing dust and pins from over here; stencils from the Manichaean guy over there; azurite, ochre and vermilion, each from a different seller for no good reason; a big sack of fine-grained clay for plaster mix, which will be hell to carry up to the caves; and, finally, father wants sketches of faces. Thirty faces, large size, detailed.

Don't be lazy, is what father said.

I know the market better than Nestis, so I will gather the supplies. Nestis draws with a firm hand, especially under pressure. He'll do the sketches. "Thirty faces, Nestis. Can you do it in an hour?" "With my eyes closed, brother." "I heard Tutuk Bugra himself is coming with his whole entourage to see the paintings." "If we miss it, we'll never be able to lift our heads," Nestis says. "Don't stop for anything." Off we go. Some of these geezer monks walk so slow I want to howl. But all I can do is bow my head and slip this way and that, a stream rushing between rocks. I leave the clay for the end and deal with paper objects first. I burst into the shops, waving a stack of stencils, shouting that *Tutuk Bugra is visiting the Cave of the Fifteen Pranidhi*, and the Master Muralist, aka my father, *needs this stuff pronto*. That snaps everyone to action. I swear it's like time speeds up. The old guys move with the speed of birds. It's beautiful to see. Their murmuring fills me with pride. "Tutuk Bugra of the Sahi family!" "Fifteen pranidhi scenes!" "That's right," I say. "And each painting is as tall as three men! In the center, there's a roof as round as the moon. My father and I decorated it by hand!" And then I'm off, onto the next item. The hardest part is pigments because, here, the enemy is me. I want to press my nose right up to the lapis lazuli and drink up every bit of color. There's a guy who deals *just* in oranges and yellows. Who knew ruddy brown could be so cheerful? Gamboge, crimson yellow, soulful maroon, reliable cinnabar. Color has infinite ways of being. I could wander the oranges forever. But my father also wants blues and reds so I'm hopping all over the place, just as he intended, having to elbow my way through this crowd of picky artisans and some gawker visitors who keep getting in my way.

The pigment guys are clever, and my boasting doesn't fool them. They take one look at the parcels slung over my shoulders and know the truth. Usted Vas says, "The Master Muralist sent you to hunt wind, eh?" His wife cracks up. "Hahaha! Your dad doesn't want you anywhere near the great dānapati. Not even a single sniff of the donor family!" She laughs so hard she cries, and her husband gently catches her tears with his blue-stained thumb. The next Usted crushes purple moss so slowly, I swear the stone of time starts rolling backwards. He yaks and yaks. "Your father carries the pure light. Yes, sing it to the heavens, the Father of Khirs is a True Uyghur Craftsman, Keeper of Ten Thousand Patterns, Draftsman of All That Is. He knows that space is the ... garment of time and the mind is the ... garment of the heart. I would give your father the ... qaba off my back, my very last dirahm, my last precious ... nugget of lapis lazuli. Gift your boots to the bootmaker even if he steals one of them, that's what I say! Am I right or ... am I right?"

This Usted prattles on and on, and obviously I can't interrupt. Everyone knows he used to have a daughter and three sons, and all of them were taken away. All I can do is humbly accept this praise on behalf of my father, and I swear it's the heaviest thing I'm carrying.

Last thing is clay. My father wants a forty-mana sack of the loamiest stuff I can find. *Forty mana!* But I decline to pay for delivery and courageously hoist this bag onto my back. I am the Thousand-Armed Avalokiteshvara with *just enough arms* to carry everything! The sun slings arrows at me. By the time I get to monastery row, I'm drooping. Luckily Nestis is easy to spot. We're both twelve, but he's weirdly tall and has the sad face of a baby Bactrian camel. The world on his back and miles to go. Nestis is hands down the best apprentice this side of the Oxos River. He was working for a guy in Qizil, copying Manichaean books he couldn't read. Some people just have the gift. He didn't think twice about leaving that workshop and joining us. He had no one to say goodbye to, no parents, no brothers or sisters, not even a stray cat. Nestis doesn't like to talk about what's gone. He's from some backwater west of Qizil, and all he owns are two palm-sized Manichaean prayer books. Praise the gods, Nestis has only managed to draw twenty-three heads so far. I drop the hulking sack of clay and flop over beside him, out of breath. "Health, my brother," Nestis says. "Peace, my son," I reply. Watching him work, it's impossible not to envy his talent, but I think I can envy Nestis with a loving heart. He really *sees* people. Their inner light and outer shadow, the heaviness of each in this world. For sure I got blessed with the Thousand Arms, but he got the Thousand Eyes. He's sketching a big guy whose badly tied gown has gone lopsided. If we sketched just his bottom half, he'd look like he was flying. Nestis fabulates. "This holy one," he says, "entered the monastery two years ago but is totally out of place. He'll leave and go into business with a food stand. See how he looks at other peoples' lunches? That's where his real happiness lives. That gentleman over there ... inherited his father's business. Sandal-maker maybe? No ... he's a barber who also does minor surgeries. He loves knives." I close my eyes and listen to him chatter. Faces emerge from the world floating behind my eyes. "Done!" Nestis says. He blows on the ink, waits for it to dry, and carefully rolls the pages up.

He hauls the sack of clay onto his back. I promise I'll carry it when we get halfway up the hill, but when the time comes, I don't do it. I'm flattened. The sun is so flaming hot, even the mountains look scorched. "Did you get everything?" Nestis says, munificently. He knows I'm on the brink of keeling over. Nestis insists that we stop and double-check my father's list. "If we forget one thing, he'll send us back for sure." He even wastes time by jiggling the pigments to make sure I bought eight ounces and not seven. He's a real friend. I say, "When you die, Nestis, I'll carry your rotting, stinking corpse across the valley and drop you off in the realm of the gods. I'll deliver melons and honey wine. You'll never be thirsty." "Thanks," he says. "Same." We load ourselves up once more and keep going. The Bezeklik, the place of paintings, rises up from the valley cliffs. This valley is for sure the gods' favorite room, a russet, walnut, yellow umber altar. Up here, I can feel the speed and eternity of god's paintbrush. Light is a memory keeper. It fills each element with something like a mind. Nestis and I paint on walls, paper and silk, but the gods paint on a sheet of time that unrolls and unrolls. "What'll they do when they see us back so fast?" "Disown us," says Nestis, which cracks us up. Sweat glues that bag of clay to his back. If he made me carry it, I'd definitely roll back down the hill. The staircases go like ladders from terrace to terrace, stretching up to the sanctuaries. Tejin fell from these heights last year and broke his arm. Put him out of commission for a chunk of time, and Nestis and I got to take over the pranidhi scene he was working on. I detailed the living daylights out of that painting. When I'm drawing, I *am* the drawing, that's how it feels. There's nothing but me and a sweet crowd of bodhisattvas, all of them happy to shoot the breeze. They call out, "Hey Khirs, my sleeve isn't right, can you make it billow a bit more?" "Fix my hair, Khirs. Make it big!" "I really want my mandorla to whirl this time!" "Khirs, Khirs, hold this flower up to the eternal." I excel at backgrounds. A background is never just a flat plane, it has to sing, just like the mountains, river and sky do all around us each and every day. On the ladder steps we pause. Nestis says, "They're already there. See the banners?" Silk blows everywhere: in the canopy that shades the assembled group, in the shine of formal hats and fancy headdresses, in the richness of gowns that move like liquid color. Gold glints in the ink-black hair of the men, and we are awestruck.

We both stop.

We're lugging parcels, wearing mud on our feet and dripping sweat. Nestis's shirt is splotched with crimson like someone knifed him. A face looms over the terrace and spots us. It's a royal attendant of some kind, and as soon as he sees us, he instantly pretends he didn't see us. Salvation. But another face pops up. A robe so beautiful it looks alive. A big shot, judging by his glorious, perfectly arranged hat. "Are you the painters?" "Yes, Venerable One." The big shot disappears and says something lost to the wind. Nestis whispers, "*Venerable* is totally wrong. He's a prince, right?" The attendant's face reappears. "Get up here. Double quick." We slog up the stairs. At the top, in front of our home, I'm temporarily blinded by so many new and incompatible things. My father, cousin, aunt and uncle, and that marmot Tejin, are not here. Instead there's this prince. One attendant holds a giant silk fan and the other holds a fly whisk, a trinity of pure color so beautiful I wish I could hold the image in my hand. To their right is the Upasthāyaka in his special-day crimson robes, flanked by three monks. The Upasthāyaka keeps his eyes half-closed as if he can't believe this is happening. Same. Completing this scene: Nestis with a forty-mana bag of loam sitting on his back like a gray hump, and me.

I have no time to ponder the whys and wherefores of this earthly life. The Fan Attendant is asking our names and functions and, simultaneously, the

Upasthāyaka is bowing low like a soft, old feather. As he falls past me, he murmurs, "Answer his lordship, the Bey Sahi." Fortunately, I'm already bent low due to the parcels which cover my body like armor. I say that I am Khirs, a painter-worker, son of the Master Muralist. "And this would be your brother?" "This," I say, staring at Nestis's worn-down sandals, "is Nestis, apprentice to our workshop." From this vantage point, I can see almost nothing. Only the sweep of the silk fan and, occasionally, the fly whisk, kicking this way and that like a horse tossing its mane. The Fan Attendant says that the Bey Sahi would like to hear more about the fifteen paintings that adorn the outer corridor of this sanctuary, so graciously commissioned by the Family Sahi. The Upasthāyaka begins to answer, but the Bey says to let the painter-workers speak. The Bey's voice is different from any sound I've ever heard. It's airy yet immovable. I inform him that the fifteen wall paintings depict the promise of the Buddha. That is, they are a sequence of fifteen pranidhi images, which surround the pilgrim on all sides, guiding them inwards to the central sanctuary. This inner room holds, beneath a dome, a sculpture and an image of the Avalokiteshvara Buddha. Bey Sahi asks me who I think Avalokiteshvara is. Of course, being my father's son, I have no trouble with this question. "Avalokiteshvara is the emanation of compassion in this world. The Thousand-Armed Thousand-Eyed Avalokiteshvara is the being who delays their longing for enlightenment in order that they might aid others in their time of suffering." I see the crimson robes of the Upasthāyaka trembling, but before he gets the chance to edify us all, the Bey Sahi says, "Did your hands paint these scenes?" "There are eight of us whose hands did the work." Even though I try to swallow the ache of pride, it wells up. "This place is the home of my father's workshop, and we have been sleeping and laboring here for three years." "Where does the workshop go when the home is completed?" "I don't know." My eyes, fixed on the floor, focus on the grains of sand blowing over my toes. These grains once belonged to the mountains, and they, too, journey immeasurable distances. Nestis shifts, and the clay he is carrying makes a falling noise without actually falling. Nestis says, "The workshop goes wherever there is work." "When you have grown old, do you think you'll return to see your work and the Buddhas you have painted?" "My father believes that we should always move forward." The shopping dangling from my body is not getting any lighter. Fatigue and annoyance make me add, "Maybe the Buddha, too, has to leave the sanctuary. Eventually."

The Bey asks someone to bring him tea. The fly whisk sings through the air, the silk fan exhales and a canister of tea appears. The Bey is so relaxed it's as if he's sitting in a grand, carpeted room. I am not a boy, I tell myself. I'm a scroll filled with images he cannot read. He says, "Do you believe that the Buddha himself resides in the paintings?" It's up to the gods to decide where they feel at home, isn't it? But what I say is, "All we can do is make the place of paintings." The Upasthāyaka says something which is not meant for my ears but travels through them anyway. The Donating Family, he is saying, the esteemed Dāna-pati and the Danka, the high members of the Family Sahi, are with the Abbot in the Temple Monastery. I see a drop of sweat fall from Nestis and bounce off the walkway, and from this I know we are thinking the same thing. One, my father and the others must be at the monastery, and when they return, Uncle Rangkar will murder us. Two, this Bey Sahi prefers to be apart. Curious. The Fly Whisk Attendant comes and takes away the parcels and the bag of clay, and tells us that we may straighten. I do, though I felt wiser when I was contemplating the dust. "Who taught you what you know?" asks the Bey Sahi. "My father guides us." "Does everyone in your family do this work?" "We are all artisans, but my sister and mother died three years ago." There are more words, but what I hear is my sister saying, *Let's go, let's go*, and feel my hand holding her painting hand while she draws a blue phoenix, and it feels as if this image is coming from a part of myself that I can't see. The Bey Sahi says, "In death, where did they go?" I cannot answer such a question. Nestis says, "They're behind the light."

The Bey laughs. His laugh is a round bouncing ball that doesn't hurt us when it strikes. I feel like a clasp has come undone in him. "Is that where the true sanctuary exists, *behind* the light?" He laughs again, but when I hear that false sound, I recognize an anger within him, or maybe an illness, and I pity him. If it were just the Bey Sahi, Nestis and me, I might tell him about the faces we sometimes see in the darkness. Images of my sister and my mother, images from Nestis's old life. Sometimes we imagine that we can set these images inside the walls of the sanctuary. Sometimes we actually do it. From all that I have seen in this world, I believe it is the privilege of the painters to light the underlying layers with a memory world. What is complete and finished belongs to the temple, the teachers, the dāna-pati and donor families, and all those who claim ownership of worldly things and objects. But I believe that everything that is unfinished is ours.

Father says that a pure heart is always prepared, always willing, to release this life. But I own an object that I would never release, not for all the precious things of this world. It's a stone with glimmering layers of azure and malachite. My older sister Altin used to hold it in her hand, even while she slept, as if holding the round hand of a round god. Two colors, mallow green and infinite blue, shine like rivers inside this rock. Altin died in the same accident as my mother. I have kept this stone ever since Father and I left Shazhou, the place where my sister first taught me to draw.

The man in front of us is afraid of many things. That's the feeling I gather from the air. He asks, "Which of you draws the faces of the pure ones and the Buddha?" "Nestis draws them." Nestis is calm as a row of stone steps. He glances up. "To paint a face is also to read it." He is ready to catch the Bey Sahi's next question even before it is asked. "All right. Tell me. What do you read in my face?" Everyone knows the Bey Sahi is actually asking a different question. *What do you see in the face that I was given, the face that I must carry, this face that is my most transitory possession?* Nestis closes his eyes and does that thing he does. He looks at the man's life. Nestis says, "I see a man of faith. A man for whom faith is the act of salvation." Bey Sahi does not know what to do with this answer. Half turning away, he says, "Aren't you afraid for your paintings?" "What do you mean?" "What becomes of them after you go away?" "We know that the color will remain for a long time, Bey Sahi." "The color?" "The pigments. Some come from leaves and roots. And some come from rocks but are not rocks themselves." "So if red ink traces the image of the Buddha, does that red ink join with the eternal and become it?"

That's a misunderstanding, I think. Eternity will never reside here.

"I don't know, Bey Sahi," says Nestis. "In these caves," the man persists, "you paint mostly in darkness, is that true? No lamps whatsoever and, only occasionally, a candle?" Nestis says, "The paintings belong to a different realm. In earthly light, they fade." I say, "That's true," and Nestis adds, "Yes." Something comes to a close. A look is exchanged which Nestis and I pretend not to understand or even notice. The Bey Sahi says something to the Upasthāyaka who says something to his monks, and time begins to move again. “I wish you health,” the Bey Sahi says, and we reply, “I wish you peace.” And then this prince of the imperial city, with his questions and his anguish, is gone. My mother used to say that the hardest thing is not that we paint Avalokiteshvara in darkness, but that we paint the gods in the presence of a weaker light. These words live in a space outside of me, just beyond my grasp. I would give anything for my mother and sister to appear, to travel beside us to the Six Cities. Each oasis town is its own apparition. But I also need them to rest where they are, safe in the place that was once our home, so that I will know how to return to them, and how to be with them again.

The next day, Father begins the final paintings, which are of the dāna-pati and donors from the great family Sahi. He tells us that the three men and two women he is painting are princes and princesses of the family, that they have suffered sorrow and are in need, as all men and women are, of peace. That is why they have dedicated their wealth to building this sanctuary in the Bezeklik. We will never know anything more about the dāna-pati, yet father has the responsibility of laying their images upon the walls.

"It is not their faces I'm painting," my father says, "but their salvation."

"How can something like that be painted?"

"It is the only thing that can be painted."

Afterwards, Nestis and I can't sleep. We find it hard to swallow the fact that next week we will be without a home. Quietly we go outside, into this night full of stars. Faint light rests on the jagged lines of the encircling mountains. I want to plant myself in this place and grow wild here forever, but instead I ask Nestis where the workshop will go next. He says he overheard my Uncle Rangkar saying that we might have a job in Hami. I tell him that I've heard that Hami is a fun place. After a while, Nestis asks, "Where do the gods keep their treasured things?" I know that he's thinking about the distance between his beginning and his end, about his parents and brothers, about their disappearance. "Do the gods keep things safe," Nestis asks, "or are they content to scatter them? Do they try to salvage what is precious, or don't they? Why are we made of the soil and the earth if the earth is not our true home?" I don't know. I think of my sister Altin and how we used to draw together on the same unrolling sheet of paper, my wrestlers leaping around her gods, my gods meditating beside her laypeople, and platters so full of grapes, melons and cucumbers that we hoped the weight of these offerings would fall through the paper and into the world. Sometimes, now, when Nestis and I paint the gods and their believers, when I watch my father and uncle and everyone mix and pattern such beautiful colors, I wonder if we are saving the gods for longevity or entrapping them in a place that can never be their home. "Probably it's both," says Nestis. "That's my guess, anyway." I look away to the hidden moon. "Same." The mirroring ink of the sky is everywhere and all things, and I feel afraid. But I keep my eyes open because I want to learn if the sky intends to swallow me or accompany me. I thank the gods for the presence of Nestis, who sees things that no one on this earth will ever see again. I send a prayer towards Altin. We are both drowsing, but I try to hold onto my mind, eye and hand. Sometimes I know this trinity, which is myself, really is a single unity.

But other times, like now, I feel them radiating out to different realms, like three travelers who will not be permitted to return home but who will recall, at moments separated by desert and sea, by future and past, the lost awareness of a once sacred unity, and the feeling of wholeness.

Afterword

The Artisans is a work of fiction imagined from the surviving fragments of Bezeklik Cave 20, a sanctuary outside the city of Turfan in present-day Xinjiang Autonomous Region, China. I wanted to pay tribute to the glorious color and expressive lines that arose from the painters' hands. I wanted to meet art with art.

I am indebted to the extraordinary, and extraordinarily moving, research of Lilla Russell-Smith, Curator of Central Asian Art, Museum für Asiatische Kunst of the Staatliche Museen zu Berlin, and to her groundbreaking book, *Uygur Patronage in Dunhuang: Regional Art Centres on the Northern Silk Road in the Tenth and Eleventh Centuries* (Leiden: Brill, 2005).

All the paintings of Bezeklik Cave 20, including the fifteen *pranidhi* paintings referred to in *The Artisans*, were removed in the Second German Turfan Exposition (1904–1905) led by Albert von Le Coq (1860–1930). Le Coq, born in Berlin, was a brewer and wine merchant who, in middle age and supported by his wealth, began to study archaeology. Aided by assistants, Le Coq cut through, carved out and removed over 360 kilograms of wall paintings, manuscripts, artifacts and other works of art from the Turfan region. Contents of the Bezeklik caves were shipped by caravan and train to Germany, where they became part of the collection of the Museum für Asiatische Kunst in Berlin.

Cave 20's fifteen *pranidhi* paintings, pieces of the ceiling and paintings from the entrances and vestibules were housed in the Königliches Museum für Völkerkunde, the ethnological museum of Berlin. During the Second World War, almost everything was destroyed in Allied bombings. Today, the main wall paintings are no more; they exist only in sketches and photographic documentation. The surviving small fragments of Cave 20—most famously, donor portraits of the Uyghur princes and princesses—can be seen at the Humboldt Forum.

The Artisans is set in or around the eleventh century, in the years of the Uyghur Kingdom of Kocho, present-day Turfan. This was a time in which Manichaean ideas, once prominent, remained in circulation but were in retreat, and Buddhism was becoming the dominant religion of the ruling elite.

Since 2017, in the Xinjiang Autonomous Region, China has interned over one million Uyghurs, Kazakhs and other Muslim minorities in secret reeducation camps and forced-labor prisons. Leaked Chinese government documents have revealed the use of extreme violence, torture and forced sterilizations to "break their lineage, break their roots, break their connections and break their origins." These prisons are now understood to be the largest arbitrary internment of ethnic and religious minorities since the Second World War.

Nearly 500,000 children are believed to have been separated from their families.

The ongoing brutality and tragedy in Xinjiang weighed on my mind as I studied, over the past five months, this fragment from Bezeklik Cave 20: the portrait of Uyghur princes and donors. This fragment was created and invested with meaning in a place that was a crossroads of beliefs, goods, languages, teachings, artistic practices, words and memory—a place that searches for salvation.

The following works of literature, poetry and reportage speak to the ongoing human rights crimes in the Xinjiang Autonomous Region.

Perhat Tursun, *The Backstreets: A Novel from Xinjiang*, trans. Darren Byler and Anonymous (New York: Columbia University Press, 2022).

Tahir Hamut Izgil, *Waiting to Be Arrested at Night: A Uyghur Poet's Memoir of China's Genocide*, trans. Joshua L. Freeman (New York: Penguin, 2023).

Ilham Tohti, *We Uyghurs Have No Say: An Imprisoned Writer Speaks* (New York: Verso, 2022).

Nury Turkel, *No Escape: The True Story of China's Genocide of the Uyghurs* (London: William Collins, 2022).

Aziz Isa Elkun, ed., *Uyghur Poems* (New York: Penguin Books, 2023).

Uyghur Collective, "Uyghur Literature in Translation," https://uyghurcollective.com/community/f/uyghur-literature-in-translation-english.

Uyghur PEN, https://www.uyghurpen.org/.

Raffi Khatchadourian, "Surviving the Crackdown in Xinjiang," *New Yorker* (April 5, 2021).

Ben Mauk, "Inside Xinjiang's Prison State," *New Yorker* (February 28, 2021).

Amy Qin, "In China's Crackdown on Muslims, Children Have Not Been Spared," *New York Times* (December 28, 2019).

Austin Ramzy and Chris Buckley, "'Absolutely No Mercy': Leaked Files Expose How China Organized Mass Detention of Muslims," *New York Times* (November 16, 2019).

Chris Buckley and Austin Ramzy, "China's Detention Camps for Muslims Turn to Forced Labor," *New York Times* (December 16, 2018).

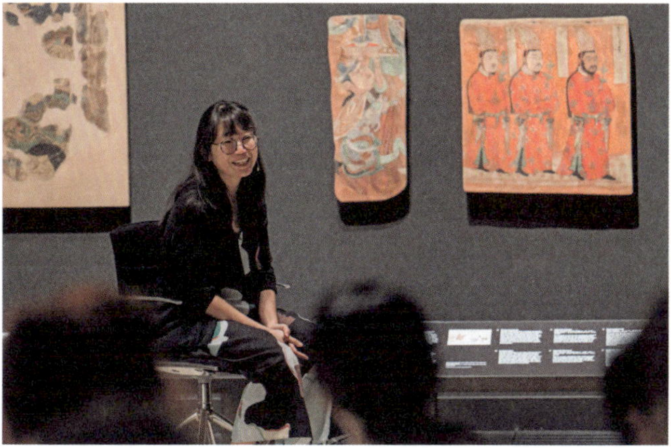

Madeleine Thien at the Humboldt Forum

OBJECTS
TALK BACK

Priya Basil
Locked In and Out
Preface by Hartmut Dorgerloh

Few buildings are as controversial as the new Berlin Palace, which now houses the Humboldt Forum. In Germany and beyond, people wonder why an imperial palace was rebuilt in the center of Berlin and then filled with the often violently acquired ethnological collections of the Prussian Cultural Heritage Foundation. The writer Priya Basil unfurls the story of the palace reconstruction alongside a personal story of her migrating to Berlin. She questions what such a building means for our understanding of the past and our sense of belonging in the present. "In German the word *Schloss* means a palace, and also a 'lock.' The central question: Can a lock also be a key?"

Meena Kandasamy
A Wise One, a Warrior
Preface by Priya Basil

The Mithuna couple is a 17th-century ivory sculpture from Tamil Nadu (India) depicting lovers. Meena Kandasamy examines how caste and class are carved into the object as indelibly as its physical details. She unfurls worlds of possibility around this seemingly idyllic couple, connecting them to personal and political stories that expose painful realities of who gets to love whom. With astonishing narrative flair—mixing X threads, academic discourse, poetry, memoir—she lets the object talk and talk back.

OBJECTS TALK BACK

Léonora Miano
Ladies of the Throne
Preface by Priya Basil

"Most of the time, it is the power of men that we remember." These words open Léonora Miano's narrative about Mandu Yenu, a throne from the ancient Kingdom of Bamum (present-day Cameroon). The Germans long claimed the object was a "gift" from King Njoya to Kaiser Wilhelm II. Miano reads "between the lines of beads and cowrie shells" to show the complexity of colonial and gender relations. She reveals that Mandu and Yenu were royal wives in the Kingdom of Bamum. The very name of the object suggests it—it is the power of women that we should remember.

Rawi Hage
The Call
Preface by Priya Basil

After one of the Turfan archaeological expeditions in the early 1900s, a fragment of a Manichaean text written in Uyghur and Old Turkic found its way to the Museum für Asiatische Kunst of the Staatliche Museen zu Berlin. Originating from the Northern Silk Road region (now the Xinjiang Uyghur Autonomous Region in China), these "fragmented leaves" became a source of inspiration for Rawi Hage: "I was born not far from Byblos, Lebanon. Ancient Byblos is considered to be the place where the first alphabet was invented." Encountering this rare and precious manuscript, with its layered and multicolored words, Hage reflects on the uprooting, displacement and migration of both objects and people.

Published by Stiftung Humboldt Forum im Berliner Schloss

Concept: Priya Basil
Project management: Katharina Kepplinger
Text editing: James Copeland
Image editing: Barbara Martinkat

Special thanks to Fränze Czaja, Han Song Hiltmann and Jan Linders (SHF) as well as to Lilla Russell-Smith (SMB) for their friendly support.

www.humboldtforum.org

Federal Government Commissioner for Culture and the Media

Funded by the Federal Government Commissioner for Culture and the Media in line with a resolution by the German Federal Parliament

 The Deutsche Nationalbibliothek lists this publication in the Deutsche Nationalbibliografie; detailed bibliographic data are available on the Internet at http://dnb.dnb.de.

ISBN 978-3-0358-0794-3
Layout: 2edit, Zurich
Printed in Germany

DIAPHANES – Schöneggstrasse 5 – CH-8004 Zurich
DIAPHANES Berlin – Dresdener Strasse 118 – 10999 Berlin – kontakt@diaphanes.net